T0198664

Forget Me Not

'A daughter's love challenged by Dementia'

DEBBIE FLACK

BALBOA.
PRESS
A DIVISION OF HAY HOUSE

Balboa Press books may be ordered through booksellers or by contacting:

Balboa Press
A Division of Hay House
1663 Liberty Drive
Bloomington, IN 47403
www.balboapress.com.au
1 (877) 407-4847

Because of the dynamic nature of the Internet, any web addresses or
links contained in this book may have changed since publication and
may no longer be valid. The views expressed in this work are solely those
of the author and do not necessarily reflect the views of the publisher,
and the publisher hereby disclaims any responsibility for them.

The author of this book does not dispense medical advice or prescribe
the use of any technique as a form of treatment for physical, emotional,
or medical problems without the advice of a physician, either directly
or indirectly. The intent of the author is only to offer information
of a general nature to help you in your quest for emotional and
spiritual well-being. In the event you use any of the information in
this book for yourself, which is your constitutional right, the author
and the publisher assume no responsibility for your actions.

Any people depicted in stock imagery provided by Thinkstock are
models, and such images are being used for illustrative purposes only.
Certain stock imagery © Thinkstock.

Print information available on the last page.

ISBN: 978-1-5043-0808-3 (sc)
ISBN: 978-1-5043-0809-0 (e)

Balboa Press rev. date: 05/08/2017

In memory of a wonderful woman, our Mum,
sister, grandmother, great grandmother and friend.

We will always remember the roll of her eyes,
her kindness and her firm, encouraging words
'Strewth', as she guided us along, pushing us
to achieve more than she could in life.

For this and much more, we thank you and honour you,

I will always love you.

The Forget me not Flower

The Forget me not plant produces small flowers with five petals.

The most familiar colour for the Forget me not flower is the blue variety. This is often found in bouquets.

Throughout history the Forget me not has been associated with remembering, lost love, as well as caring for the poor and disabled.

The Alzheimer's Association have also used this flower as a symbol to represent memory loss and the remembrance of loved ones who have passed on due to this disease.

Introduction

Memories make us who we are they say. What happens when we can't recall any?

……… … Our loved ones help us.

At the time of writing it is nearing Mother's Day once again. Mum has been gone a little over a year. I reflect on something Mum used to reply when asked

"What would you like for Mother's Day?"

"Peace of mind" she would sigh.

How true the meaning of this would come to be many years later.

Dementia describes a collection of symptoms that are caused by disorders affecting the brain. It is not one specific disease[1]. No matter what type of dementia a person has, the journey for the sufferer and their loved ones can truly be a difficult one.

Along the way I struggled to find answers to our never-ending stream of questions. Some people listened and cared but many others unfortunately were ignorant,

---

[1] Alzheimers Australia website

too busy or 'it's not my department' to help us live day by day with dementia. By reading this book you too are probably on the search for answers and understanding. I hope you will find this book of some help and comfort as you continue your journey. You are not alone. Scour the internet for websites that may be of assistance. I would highly recommend

www.fightdementia.org.au and **Alzheimers Australia (Qld).**

1

2006

I distinctly remember the coloured rays of light filtering through the thin blinds in the hospital waiting room. Mum seemed to be taking a while to come out. The doctor finally appeared asking to speak to both Mum and I.

In a tiny nondescript room he opened a manila folder with Mum's name neatly adhered to the top and showed us photographs of a large evil-looking growth which they had found during a routine colonoscopy. His voice seemed to fade away into the distance, until I noticed that he was looking at our faces, waiting for the answer to a question he obviously had just asked. Making the decision himself he made a call to a specialist upstairs and booked an appointment for us to see him in one hour's time.

It was decided that in three days, Mum would have a major operation to remove the growth and a length of her bowel including lymph nodes. Leaving the specialist office we walked in stunned silence to the car and returned home. Those three days dragged. I rang my younger brother and sister, who both lived interstate, as well as a couple of Mum's friends and sisters plus my adult children. Emotions ran high. Mum sat alone in her house all weekend with her thoughts and fears, not wanting to make the calls herself.

On the morning of the operation we were understandably nervous. They took Mum away and I waited and waited until the doctor gave me the results. The operation was a success! Thank goodness.

However, after the operation, Mum started saying bizarre things. She didn't realize that she was in hospital and had an operation. Medical staff said

"It's probably just the anesthetic. Once it's out of her system she'll be alright."

I wondered …

The year was 2006. Looking back, I feel this was the first evidence of that cruel disease dementia invading Mum's mind.

2

OUR FAMILY

On average, families with the skill of hindsight, acknowledge that they noticed symptoms of Dementia three years before a proper diagnosis was made.

This was true of Mum. Like the edges of a cloth starting to fray, Mum's personality and understanding of situations started to change. I had attributed the uncertainty which Mum displayed in decision making, plus the heavier reliance on me, due to her traumatic cancer operation and living alone.

Mum was also getting older, wasn't she?

Mum was born in 1934 and lived in the Murrarie and Morningside areas of South Brisbane. She was the eldest of eleven children and so as she became older, she was responsible for many of the daily chores within the household. As each new sibling was born, she helped care for the other children and cleaned the house. This was a common occurrence in families of that time. Mum received good results in school. This was an even greater achievement, due to the fact that with every new baby born, she would be absent from school for some time. As time passed, Mum started working in Brisbane city. With money saved she enjoyed buying smartly coordinated outfits for going out with her work friends and sisters.

She attracted the eye of my handsome dark haired father who was living at West End, South Brisbane. On Valentine's Day 1953 they married and lived for a short time with Dad's family. After I was born we moved to a small one bedroom flat in Highgate Hill, South Brisbane. Most of my memories of that place are blurred but I can remember fondly a neighbour I called 'Mrs Bish'. Apparently at a prescribed time most mornings, I would totter up the stairs to Mrs Fisher's place for morning tea being careful not to disturb the scary cats which hid under the stairway. Even then I displayed an independent streak.

Another memory I recall vividly, was when sitting in the warm alcove of our bay window, I was alerted to the sounds of drums and trumpets playing. I looked out to see a circus parading past. Excitedly I shouted, "Look Mum, a circus!" I strained to watch them as they travelled further down the steep road into the heart of Brisbane. That same road also held a frightening memory for my Uncle Alan. Being my father's younger brother, Alan remembers sitting on the front handlebars of Dad's bicycle, white faced and hands tightly clenched, as Dad pedaled as fast as he could down the steep busy road yelling at the top of his lungs. Dad delighted in the thrill of this 'high jinx'. Uncle Alan was not as impressed.

My brother was born two years after me. Our family was expanding so Mum and Dad decided to find a house we could call home. In the new suburb of West Chermside, on the north side of Brisbane, surrounded by bush and connected to civilization by a dusty road, they worked hard to establish a modest home with a mortgage.

From a young age, I remember many a weekend spent helping Mum and Dad cart large boulders from the backyard to the unlevelled front yard. Grass was laid, shrubs planted and wooden floors were varnished. Our home was complete.

Mum was quite a proud woman. She would often take us, the kids, to visit Dad's parents. We would be dressed immaculately in our best clothes and were always reminded of our manners. We didn't visit Mum's family which I always thought was strange but as we didn't have a car or phone, I imagined that their home was too difficult to reach by public transport.

It would take us most of the day to travel to and from West End, South Brisbane. Catching a bus or taxi to the tram terminus we would then travel into Brisbane city. There we would walk to catch another tram to cross the Brisbane River to West End.

Trams always fascinated and scared me. On one trip, I must have been wriggling in my seat as one of my sandals came off and landed on the top step of the tram. Mum was angry with me for being so careless and made me climb down off my seat when the tram stopped to collect my shoe. I was so scared of falling out of the tram.

Once arriving at our stop, we would then walk what seemed a long way with our little legs to Grandma's house.

Our Grandparents' house was a relatively small wooden place where people came and went all the time. It was a house where little children were seen and definitely not heard. Grandfather was a strong, stern, white-haired man who commanded the top seat of the kitchen table at lunch time. I think we were too scared to be naughty. Often when Grandfather was not there, one of Dad's older brothers came over for lunch. He had us in fits of laughter with his funny jokes and facial expressions as he ate his lunch of baked bean sandwiches which were all neatly wrapped in waxed paper. Grandma busied herself around the kitchen during his visits. She also seemed to like his relaxed banter. He seemed such a contrast to Grandfather.

Before long it was time to start our long journey home. I often envied my brother and sister as they rode in the stroller or were carried by Mum. They must have been long weary days for Mum.

By the time my sister was born, my brother and I were both in Primary School. My father's job was in the city and so he would have to leave early in the morning to catch his bus and tram. He was good at his job. He had the *'gift of the gab'* and could often convince the female customers to purchase an extra towel or sheet from his Manchester department. After work he would enjoy a drink or two with his mates before returning home on the last bus at night. We didn't see Dad very much then except on weekends when he would often join us in a short game of backyard cricket. Those years would have been very lonely for Mum also. Our neighbours were very good, and chats at the backyard fence were a common occurrence and a form of relaxation and communication for Mum.

Growing up, my brother and I spent long hours in the back yard playing *'chasey'*, cricket and kicking the football. We had fun together. Playing in the house was only for wet days and then we drove Mum crazy. At other times, I loved to quietly make cards and booklets using paper, pictures from magazines and coloured pencils. I would make an assortment and give them to our neighbours as presents.

When I was seven I was so excited to have a little sister. I would try to look after her, but she wriggled a lot and she would often bite me so I learnt not to cuddle her too tight or for too long. One morning before school Mum was cooking Dad's breakfast and I had to take my sister into the lounge and keep her there. Wriggling to get away, I lost my grip. She fell, landing on the floor screaming. Both of my parents rushed in, angry with me. Mum, or 'the belt' was usually the disciplinarian in our household. Once everyone calmed down I was allowed out of my room.

The nature of Dad's employment changed. He became head salesman. In those days a client would be taken out for dinner and over a couple of drinks, the business deals were finalized. This style of business with excessive smoking and drinking placed an incredible strain on finances and relationships. The following years were difficult ones especially between Mum and Dad. As the eldest I remember quite clearly my parents' constant arguments.

When my sister started Primary School, Mum worked for a few hours in the evenings and on Saturdays at the local TAB. This helped financially and gave Mum a social release. I was left in charge to finish cooking tea, look after my brother and sister and have everything neat, tidy and quiet for when my father came home from work. During those years, my father always seemed to be drinking. He was very critical of everything Mum or I did. Annoyed at me he would yell, *"You're just like your mother!"*

Interestingly Mum would often worry about leaving me with my father because of our clashes. She thought I was too much like him in personality. Looking back with more mature eyes now, I can see how unhappy both of my parents must have been. The destructive influence of alcohol didn't help the situation.

As the years passed, my sister and I both married young and left home. My brother married a few years later. This left Mum and Dad alone together. Dad continued to drink. Divorce was not an option then.

When grandchildren came along this lightened the atmosphere. Mum enjoyed hearing about their latest antics and achievements. She would proudly display the latest photos of all the grandchildren and brag about them to the ladies and customers at the TAB.

Grandma
With red blistered hands
She lovingly knits
A brand new bonnet
For the latest arrival.

Her heart swells in adoration
As she gazes across
The framed sea of faces
On the polished tabletop.

Rejoicing with loved ones
She proudly displays
The tenderness felt
For her precious family.

3

Dribbling from the right side of his mouth, painstakingly Dad raised a trembling hand as he tried to eat his cereal. Almost overnight, Dad who was only sixty-five, started to display the physical signs of a stroke. After tests, it was revealed that he had an aggressive secondary brain cancer which most likely had stemmed from a large sun cancer my father had stubbornly refused to have properly removed a year earlier. Mum cared for him at home as best as she could for three months as his health deteriorated. Even during this time, their relationship didn't change. Maybe it was too late for them, I don't know. He was in unbearable physical pain which added to his frustration and anger. For the final two weeks of his life he was moved into Palliative care.

He passed away late January 1999. My sister was living in Sydney at the time. Later that year my brother moved interstate with his wife. With my father gone, Mum initially kept herself busy by working in the garden and refurnishing the house to reflect her own tastes. As we later realized though, she struggled to move on with her life.

One of her sisters would invite her out to the movies

or meet up for a *'cuppa'*. I tried to encourage her into craft or social group outings but to no avail. We managed to get Mum on a plane twice to visit her daughter and family in Sydney. Although she enjoyed seeing them, she became more and more anxious about traveling anywhere. Unfortunately, she never gave herself a chance to see her son and his family in Melbourne. Sad for both mother and son.

Gradually Mum started to decline invitations for outings. Even conversations with her neighbours of forty years started to become strained. I became Mum's social life. The neighbours would often see my 'little red car' pull up to take Mum out for the day.

My son remembers fondly taking Grandma out for her birthday. Mum would always insist on paying for things even when it was a gift for her. My son wanted to buy her some books as she enjoyed reading. After some friendly banter and a slap from his Grandmother, my son a well-built young man, paid for the books whilst his much shorter grey haired Grandma told him quite adamantly that she would pay for their morning tea. Subject closed.

Niggling pains and frequent visits to the doctor became common for Mum. After one such visit, an appointment was made for a colonoscopy. Bowel Cancer! The year was 2006.

Mum and I had always had a close relationship. This often comes with being the eldest child. The news of her impending bowel operation formed an even stronger bond which proved to be significant in her future.

4

2007

Months later, after recovering from her operation, Mum's phone calls which were usually long in duration, became increasingly more emotional. My son who was living with me at the time, would often make me a cup of tea when he knew it was Grandma on the phone. One work morning Mum rang me at 5:00 very upset. She was unable to tell me what was wrong. She was very distressed, even hinting at self-harming. She begged me to come over. Like a crazy woman I drove to Mums. It took over an hour to calm her down. I could not see anything wrong or out of place. At the time I had no idea what could have triggered such a reaction from her. Once normality resumed, I travelled to work feeling very confused and shaken by the events. I rang my son to reassure him that everything was alright and rang Mum later in the day to check on her only to be told,

"I'm alright, why are you ringing?"

Not long after, at the happy occasion of my daughter's wedding I found myself asking, *"Who is this woman?"* Mum's manner was usually that of a quiet lady but she

11

turned into an abusive alcohol guzzling woman. My brother and sister who had travelled up for the wedding were very concerned when they escorted Mum home. After resting for a couple of days, Mum returned to normal. We thought the unusual behaviour was just the combination of medication, excitement of the day and not eating enough food. Mum had never eaten well. My brother could not recall a time when we were growing up, when he saw Mum eat. She always made sure her family had enough to eat first before she would consider eating herself. This is something a lot of mothers do.

Mum was becoming more confused and anxious about many things in her daily life. She needed help. Somehow I had to spend more time with her, but how? I needed a job with more flexible hours. In the stressful job of teaching there was always a mountain of 'homework' which had to be completed. I decided that I could not combine teaching, helping Mum and loving my family successfully together, so I left teaching. Unfortunately, with an unstable job market I had three jobs in two years. This added to my stress. Eventually I gained a part-time job in retail, where I worked in the evenings.

In May 2009, I was married for the second time. Although it was a relaxed garden wedding, Mum's anxiety was high once again. She seemed stressed that all her family, children, grandchildren and great grandchildren, were coming together for the happy occasion. At one stage, she even refused to attend the wedding which was both bizarre and distressing for me. Eventually she attended and seemed relaxed enjoying the company of her grandchildren. It was noticeable however, that she had lost a considerable amount of weight over a short space of time. Once again, I thought it was the combination of not eating and stress that contributed to the weight loss and strange behaviour. A few days later Mum appeared relaxed and her normal self once more.

Alarm bells had started to ring.
What was happening?

5

2010

In the early afternoon at a local café, I sat with Mum sharing a *'cuppa'*. From the *'outside looking in'* it appeared to be a lovely scene, but not all was as it seemed. It was now four years since Mum's cancer operation.

As an almost weekly event Mum and I would sit in a familiar café and chatter away about the family, grandchildren and current events whilst enjoying a coffee and toasted sandwiches. However, the flow of conversation now had transformed into a series of repetitive questions and a vagueness interlaced with emotional surges.

Mum was losing weight. She often did not finish her meals complaining about the taste and quality of the food or coffee. She would tire quickly in the afternoons, requiring me to take her elbow when walking. This helped to maintain her balance and guide her through what was once a familiar place to shop. We avoided the noisy areas as this seemed to aggravate her. She was looking tired and drawn, much older than her years.

As Mum tired she would become confused and anxious. She would start to question repetitively,

"How will I get home?
Do you know where I live?
Will you take me home?"
Then she would cry.
Inside, my heart would also drop.

At the café, other noticeable changes were occurring. The normal banter about who was going to pay the bill didn't occur. Once very quick minded with calculations, Mum was becoming increasingly vague about the value of coins. To disguise this problem, she would often pass over a note, one from the security of her bra, rather than counting out coins.

I was beginning to find large amounts of money in secret hiding spots around her house. I started to realize that Mum was frequently withdrawing large sums of money from the local bank and not remembering her visits. After trying to discuss this with Mum it was decided that I would accompany Mum to the bank after our weekly 'coffee' at the café.

I had no authority however to intervene with her transactions when I thought she was withdrawing too much money. I had to help Mum keep track of her money without embarrassing her.

At the same time, by pure chance, I intercepted some phone calls and unusual bills. I discovered that Mum had changed her Energy Provider and had lost money in the changeover. A couple of Energy salesmen had knocked on Mum's door one day and convinced her to change providers. At the time they weren't even aware that she used gas for cooking and heating. I proceeded to clear up the mess. Mum also started to tell stories of other strangers coming to her door promoting their goods and services. She even allowed a couple of older men to enter her house. This was so out of character. Haunting me also, were stories from the media where the elderly had been taken advantage of and worse still, harmed.

It's amazing how others including family, didn't notice the changes that were happening to Mum. They were so obvious to me.

It frustrated me and I needed to find out what and why this was happening to Mum. I spoke to Mum about her tiredness and weight loss. Tackling important conversations was always best attempted in the morning, as afternoons were a minefield of emotions. Mum acknowledged that something was not quite right and so we made an appointment with her doctor. I also asked Mum if I could sit with her when the doctor spoke to her.

After exchanging pleasantries with the doctor, Mum was asked the purpose of the visit. After a pause Mum replied,

"To get another script."

Consulting Mum's records the doctor reported that Mum should have plenty of tablets left. Mum had high blood pressure and cholesterol. Mum became flustered. I tried to intercede with *"You wanted to talk to the doctor about how you have been feeling lately."* Mum looked blankly at me. The doctor started to enquire further but Mum 'shut up shop' and wanted to leave. I started to talk to the doctor but the doctor informed me that she couldn't discuss Mum's medical concerns due to Doctor-Patient confidentiality.

"But I'm her daughter!"

"Deb let's go!" Mum's voice abruptly interjected.

This was my first insight into the stumbling blocks of bureaucracy. I decided to make an appointment to see Mum's doctor on my own, and try to state my case for concern. The doctor again stated confidentiality but I was able to provide her with some of Mum's symptoms. I asked her for guidance. The doctor side tracked and asked about my state of mind and if I wanted any anti-depressants. I wasn't impressed.

She did however ask if Mum had an **Advance Health Directive**. I had no idea what it was. She explained it was a form which gives directions to medical staff as to a person's future health requirements, should they for any reason, be unable to make decisions eg. in a coma. I was told that I could pick one up from the newsagent or local post office.

Looking at the form I wondered how I was going to approach Mum with this. Early one morning, I began a conversation with her concerning her health and using a small white lie, relayed that the doctor had mentioned this form on *her* previous visit. After a lot of talk and trying to calm Mum of any concerns, boxes were ticked and appropriate places signed on the form. My brother and sister who lived interstate also signed, before getting it formally signed by a Justice of the Peace. A Commissioner for Declarations, a lawyer or a notary public would also be regarded as a 'qualified witness.'

I was so relieved that we were able to complete this form for Mum. At the time, I thought that was the most difficult conversation I could have with my Mum.

How naive I was.

6

I still needed help for Mum with her memory issues and emotional behaviour. I Googled again and found the following resources:

fightdementia.org.au
qld.fightdementia.org.au
National Dementia Hotline Helpline 1800 100 500
www.myagedcare.gov.au

Thank goodness I stumbled across these. Today the websites and resources have been updated and developed further to provide a variety of information and further links to other services. I highly recommend anyone also on this journey to 'bookmark' these sites on your computers, phones etc.

My husband and I attended a very informative but daunting seminar on Dementia. This seminar reinforced the need to get organized and become prepared for the journey. It was going to be tough.

The lecturer also made us aware of the amount of stress and strain which could be placed on relationships, especially for couples, who were helping their loved ones with Dementia.

From the seminar, we realized that the next crucial step was to have Mum assessed, but the *how* and *where* wasn't clear. As the doctor seemed unconvinced of the problems Mum was having at home, I made a series of calls to Community Health and Aged Care. An appointment was made for Mum to have an Aged Care Assessment Test (ACAT) done at home, in six weeks' time. It seemed such a long time to wait especially as Mum's symptoms were escalating.

In 2010 other forms needed to be completed. The **Enduring Power of Attorney** EPOA (short form) was also found at the Post office or Newsagent. This document is used to appoint an attorney/s for both financial matters and personal matters (including health care). This document must be completed *whilst the nominee was still with* **sound mind**.

Mum had always tried to treat, love and care for her three children equally and so she naturally decided that the three of us would be her attorneys equally, to make decisions together when the time came to do so. It was also decided that as I lived close to Mum and not interstate, when decisions of a local nature or when time was of the essence, after consultation with my brother and sister I could sign alone. Legal matters such as the sale of her house etcetera had to have our three signatures. All this was stated on the EPOA document with each of our signatures witnessed by a Justice of the Peace.

I carried these documents and also certified copies in a special folder to the various medical, financial, nursing facilities and Centrelink appointments that I/we had during the subsequent years. Centrelink was another 'fun' place to communicate with. Some people were extremely helpful but others … My questions were often *'not their department'*. Waiting on the phone for long periods of time increased my frustration. A form from Centrelink that was very helpful in the early stages was one where I became Mum's 'nominee.' By signing this, Mum gave me permission to communicate with Centrelink on her behalf. Often other organizations such as Energy companies, acknowledged this form.

Whilst I was organizing all the paperwork, Mum appeared to become more disoriented. One of Mum's neighbours alerted me to an incident where he found Mum on the ground early one morning. She appeared dazed and unsure as to why she fell. After this I exchanged phone numbers with both her neighbours in case of future accidents.

On another occasion Mum, when opening her door, appeared with grazes on her face as well as her hands and knees. In those days Mum would apply a bright yellow healing ointment onto any abrasions, so I was doubly shocked to see these coloured patches over her red raw skin. After asking what had happened, Mum appeared both vague and embarrassed. Her recollection of events seemed confusing. She said that she had tripped on the curbing when rushing to cross the busy road, outside her house, to go to the local shop. Mum had been crossing this road for many years without incident. I was worried.

This was unusual. Two falls, that I knew of, in a short space of time. I wanted to take her to the doctor but she refused, saying she would have to be more careful when crossing the road in future.

During this time there was a large amount of publicity concerning the health of public figure, Hazel Hawke. She was the first wife to a former Prime Minister of Australia and was very well liked by the public. Hazel's daughter had written a book on the initial stages of her mother's journey with Alzheimer's. I read it with mixed feelings. It highlighted for me that everyone's journey although similar is different. Even with Hazel's high profile and close living arrangements with her daughter's family, they were also struggling to cope with the day to day life of Alzheimer's. If my suspicion about Mum's health was correct, how were *we* going to cope with this disease?

Over the next couple of weeks we regularly visited the doctor. Mum's façade started to slip. At times she displayed difficulties in following the doctor's conversation, often providing bizarre responses to questions. Mum's attitude towards the doctor became hostile. The doctor observed these changes in Mum's behaviour also and diagnosed Mum to be in the initial stages of Alzheimer's.

Although my suspicions were confirmed, the diagnosis still came as a shock. Shaken, I foolishly asked, *"When will she get better?"*

"She won't!" the doctor replied.

Like a woman possessed, I read anything and everything connected with Dementia or Alzheimer's. This was paramount for Mum's future and my survival as her carer. I am sure my siblings questioned my state of mind during this time as I would email updates to them on Mum's medical appointments, cycle of symptoms and often erratic behaviour.

7

A shrill noise pulsated through my weary head. I turned and looked at the highlighted time. 1:00 am. I had only been asleep thirty minutes after working the late shift. The noise alerted me once more. The Phone! I quickly jumped out of bed and ran to the phone before it stopped.

"I've been robbed! They've taken my purse!"

The hysterical voice cried into the phone.

"When? Who?" I replied.

"Now! It was the little blonde girl. Can you come over? She might come back. Pleeease."

What followed for the next forty minutes was the interplay of broken conversations which swung from reality to the not so real. I tried to convince Mum that after she checked and re-checked her front door to see if it was locked, that she would be safe. It was still dark so I promised I would come over when the sun came up in the morning. I hoped that I could get a couple more hours sleep before the merry-go-round started again.

This scene had unfortunately become common place. Her purse had not been stolen. It was simply hidden from view. Her view. She had placed it in a 'safe' place possibly only minutes prior to the phone call, but she had forgotten. The *blonde girl* was in her mind, maybe an image she had resurrected from her past.

Mum still hadn't been assessed for ACAT, but the appointment was getting closer. Her doctor was becoming used to *our* visits and started to question Mum more on her day to day living. This would often anger Mum and she would refuse to visit the doctor again. Around this time Mum became quite disoriented. She boarded the wrong bus, got off the wrong stop, and got lost in the local shopping centre. Luckily on all occasions, *'good Samaritans'* came to Mum's rescue helping her return home safely. Inside Mum's purse I placed my contact details. I also managed to get an ID bracelet which was linked to my details. Mum however, managed to remove this bracelet. Today there appears to be more advanced models of ID bracelets available. On the internet you can find ones which have a perimeter alert, an emergency alert button, inbound mobile phone and GPS tracking locator as well as a lockable clip on the strap. These devices help ease the concerns of the carer as well as aid the wearer when they find themselves in stressful situations.

Security became an obsession with Mum. Like someone with OCD tendencies she would check the lock on the front door, opening and closing it repeatedly during the course of the evening. The lock became broken and with the assistance of the local *Community Health* organization, a locksmith replaced the broken lock with a similar one. Although safer Mum did not understand how this lock operated. She could not understand how it became unlocked when she opened it from the inside.

She thought someone else must be opening her door. The *little blonde girl* was to blame.

On a couple of occasions at night I would have to go downstairs with Mum, with torch in hand to check on the bolted laundry door. Reassured, Mum would calm down, return to bed and sleep a little longer.

As part of her security, Mum would hide her house keys, but then forget where they were placed. Eventually I had three sets of keys made: one for her use, one to be 'hidden' and one set for me. Unfortunately, Mum collected any keys she found: old ones, wardrobe keys and padlock keys. With this collection of keys she became even more confused. At this time, I bought her a bright red lanyard to place the correct door keys on. I thought, with the lanyard around her neck it would help her remember where the keys were at all times. However, the keys became lost in Mum's mind, when the lanyard sat under her clothes, out of sight. Hearing a *jingling noise of the keys when she walked* didn't make Mum any more aware of the keys location.

Also on the security front, Mum wanted to find all her legal papers. She wanted to be reassured that she owned her house and the land. I think her will, her birth certificate as well as her father's and husband's death certificates reminded her of who she was. In later months, I had to smuggle these papers away from her as she began cutting paper up into tiny shreds in the evening, so no one could read her information. In the morning however, she wouldn't remember doing this and accused people, often me or *the blonde girl*, of coming in and cutting up the paper.

The afternoons and evenings were the worst times of day for Mum. Overcast days had similar effects on her. She would appear more confused, easily agitated, and very emotional or in a depressed-like state. This I came to learn was called *Sundowning*.

8

Sept 2010

The morning of the ACAT assessment arrived. I had to prepare Mum that a stranger would enter her house and ask her questions. I had to be very careful with my wording so I didn't stress or alarm her further.

I had mixed feelings about this testing. On one hand, I wanted Mum to get all the answers right so that she wouldn't have this disease, but I also wanted her to 'slip up' so we could get some help. I was concerned how a simple ten-minute test administered by a stranger could change the course of peoples' lives. Waiting for the assessor was nerve racking for both of us.

Would Mum show her true behaviour?

What if they didn't really find anything wrong?

Would I then feel like it was me that should be assessed?

One of the most annoying and frustrating factors that most carers will acknowledge, is that the sufferer can *'put on a face'*. They can give a positive 'performance' when placed in front of a medical assessment team and asked about their memory or completion of daily tasks.

By providing simple yes/no answers and frequently used phrases or one-liners, Mum appeared to understand and respond well to the series of questions being asked. Fanciful stories were fabricated to back up answers, once again leaving me lost for words. I tried to intervene with some reality but the assessor was only listening to Mum. I started to feel sick.

After 10–15 minutes the quietly spoken assessor viewed Mum's house for future safety problems eg. rails to assist in the bathroom as well as the condition and number of steps around the house. During this time, Mum released from questioning, was pottering idly around. Usually after a doctor's appointment, Mum would be exhausted from trying to concentrate on conversations and that day was no different.

The assessor then asked how I thought Mum was going. I quickly told her some truths and my concerns. The assessor couldn't help me further but said she would pass on my concerns to her supervisor. Mum would then be assessed by the supervisor and an *ACAT level* would be allocated to her. The results of the ACAT assessment would arrive in the mail a few weeks later. I was told to keep this form as it would be very important in the future.

Again we had to wait. *What was the next step?*

9

Who am I?

My relationship with Mum was starting to change. What was our relationship? At times Mum didn't seem to know who I was.

Was I Deb her daughter or her friend?

My husband would chuckle and say *"Twins"* when Mum would provide me with a pair of pink fluffy scuffs and a long winter nightie, just like hers, when I would sleep over.

In the evening, during *Sundowning*, I would be Mum's enemy. I was someone who was bossy, stole her belongings and was always too busy at work to visit her. She would frequently call me at night on speed dial at 11:01, 11:05, 11:10pm etcetera, slamming the phone down once she had told me how annoyed she was with me. I was the one who made her angry. I made her cry. She started to phone her friend, a sister, an Aged care support number, wrong numbers and even the police, all late at night or in the early hours of the morning complaining about me.

It was explained to me that the main carer, me, was

the 'safe person' that they could express their anger and frustration towards. It didn't make me feel any better though. I was having a difficult time dealing with this person, my mother. My relationship with my husband had become very strained. I felt isolated. I was trying extremely hard to care for Mum and her mood changes. If she didn't think I was her daughter, who was I? My Mum was disappearing and my marriage was crumbling. I often found myself on the verge of tears.

Growing up I was not a confident child. As the eldest, there were rules and responsibilities. At school I struggled to learn. Thankfully, my Year 5 teacher, ignited in me a passion to learn and an interest in sketching. In Year 7 I participated in school sport. Playing sport in high school became a refuge for me from the emotional turbulence of home life.

On completion of high school, I decided to teach, as I felt I could relate to the struggle others also had when learning. At teacher's college I met my first husband. Through teaching I thrived. My confidence, knowledge, emotional maturity and creativity increased. For many years I taught children with special needs as well as mainstream students. I trained sporting teams and organized leadership and humanitarian events at my various schools.

During this time my two beautiful children were born. Back problems plagued both my husband and I. One of my operations failed miserably. Nerve damage meant that I had to learn to walk properly again. With great determination and months of hard work I was able to return to teaching, although initially it was only on a part-time basis.

While our children were still in Primary school, my husband and I separated. Our marriage of nearly twenty years had ended.

Everyone has challenges in life and I thought that this was the extent of my challenges ...

Resilience
An inner strength
That keeps you going
Even when you feel you cannot continue
Resilience

10

2010 continues.

Often unaware of the night's emotions or phone calls, Mum would start most days with a *'clean slate'*. I on the other hand had to deal with distressed friends, family and the police when they followed up on Mum's phone calls. The police recorded my details as well as details of Mum's doctor. Luckily they believed my husband and me.

Throughout this time I was lucky to have a very good friend to go walking with along the waterfront once a week. She listened and we talked about my concerns. Our strong friendship combined with the positive effects of the water, nature and exercise helped me enormously. I was able to mentally and physically escape the situation for a short time. I would highly recommend that people find the time and their own 'outlet', for the sake of their sanity.

The doctor was beginning to see further evidence of Mum's increased anxiety during her appointments, and with my persistent questioning about what to do with *'the little blonde girl'*, medication was prescribed to calm Mum down. I really didn't notice any change in emotions, but due to some side effects, the medication was later stopped.

I had to remind myself that this person was still my Mum. She must have been feeling very disoriented, scared and confused for her to react as she did. Through Community Health I managed to arrange an appointment with Mental Health for a cognitive test to take place. The test consisted of approximately fifteen questions which dealt with language, counting, time and spatial awareness drawings. A score was calculated and recorded for future tests to be compared with. A brain scan was also taken. From the scan they looked for any medical abnormalities, previous strokes or shrinkage of the brain. It was decided to start Mum on tablets to try to slow down the progress of Alzheimer's. I felt like someone was trying to help me. Our appointments with this 'memory' doctor were very important throughout this stage.

It wasn't just me Mum was suspicious of. She started telling stories of children opening her letterbox and stealing her mail. To stop the naughty children taking her letters, Mum would look in the letterbox several times a day or sit on the front steps and wait for the '*postie*' to ride past. Her paranoia about people reading her mail, also made her hide it or worse still, cut up her mail so no one could read it. This led to overdue and unpaid bills.

I organized a Post Office Box so I could collect her mail and start paying the bills. This also involved legally identifying myself to Mum's bank to organize an account through which I could pay her bills. As I was Power of Attorney equally with my brother and sister they also had to provide their details to the bank before the new account could be organized.

Every day I was rushing. I drove to and from home,

to work and then to Mum's place constantly organizing things for her. I would sit with Mum coiled ready for action or rather the next reaction in Mum's personality. It was mentally exhausting. The combination of everything as well as disturbed sleep from Mum's frequent phone calls meant I was becomingly seriously fatigued.

I needed some help.

Finally a copy of the ACAT Assessment arrived. The level, at the time of writing, would be either low or high. Mum was assessed as being *Low Level*. The ACAT assessment is critical when applying for a bed in a nursing care facility. It determines how much care would be necessary for the health and safety of the individual. I was told to keep this form somewhere safe so we could use it later. With so much happening in the present, it was difficult or naïve of me to think of what was going to happen further down the track.

11

January 2011

> *"Hi Deb, Our paranoid mother is after you.*
> *Be warned!*
> *Let me know how you go at the doctors on Tuesday.*
> *Good Luck!"*

I received this message on a Sunday night from my sister in Sydney, after I finished work for the weekend.

In the weeks which had followed Christmas, she had been receiving a barrage of calls from Mum similar to the ones I had also received. Mum's calls were highly emotional, accusing the blonde girl and me of conspiring to take her household items, bank book as well as paying her bills. She was also angry that no one came to visit her at Christmas.

In reality on Christmas Day, my brother and sister both contacted Mum with messages of love. I visited Mum on Christmas Eve with all my family, bringing with us all the food and paper plates required for a family celebration. I did this so Mum would not have to worry about anything. Photos were taken of Mum with various family members. The great-grandchildren also sat quietly with her in the lounge. Together they quietly chatted and read books. I called Mum on Christmas Day as part of my daily ritual. Mum remembered nothing. She felt dejected, all alone. I was to blame.

What a way to start the New Year!

On Mum's second visit to the Memory doctor they realized after testing, that the tablets they had recommended were not having any effect. They wanted Mum to wear a medicated patch on her shoulder which had to be changed daily. A couple of months earlier, Mum's GP had prescribed tablets to help with her paranoia, pain and to also help stimulate her appetite, as again her weight was plummeting. The Memory clinic did not want Mum to continue with these tablets due to their combination and long term side effects.

All of Mum's symptoms had increased in frequency. Her behaviour was becoming more bizarre and quite emotionally aggressive, particularly to me. This was to become a *"Year of Hell"* for me.

I also became very concerned about Mum's ability to live alone.

One afternoon upon entering her home the strong smell of burnt charcoal hit me in the face. The microwave door was open. It had several scorch marks over its interior.

"There's something wrong with the microwave," Mum replied when asked.

This occurred once again when Mum entered the wrong number values and completely melted the container and its contents. Luckily for everyone Mum had not used her gas stove for a couple of years, so as a precaution, I decided to get it turned off at the main switch.

Mum's comprehension of how to use basic electrical equipment had become non-existent. The familiar radio with an on/off button was too difficult for her to operate. She often made excuses as to why the appliances weren't working. She forgot how to use the washing machine. Handwashing her underwear and house dress in the bathroom sink became part of her daily routine. She would then hang them up under the house so the neighbours wouldn't notice. Possibly she didn't want the neighbours to find out she was having some difficulties. It was like a secret that supposedly only I was allowed to know. She was a very proud woman.

Mum's pride and stubbornness, was not a good combination at times. She was adamant that no one was going to come into her house to 'help her' do basic cleaning or shopping. Many 'community assistance services' do provide help to people in these areas. In a way, I could understand her feelings, but it meant that I continued to run two households, Mum's and my own.

Normally a quiet, polite person especially in public, she now became easily irritated and detested waiting in queues at checkouts. Loudly speaking her mind, she would often react to any incompetence or errors with a derogatory remark. I found myself cringing and hastily moving Mum along and out of the stores.

Mum wore glasses mostly for reading, so making sure she had them on and they were clean helped considerably with her vision. In the shopping centres walking across the various coloured floor surfaces would sometimes cause

Mum to falter. Moving to a dark coloured area she would stop, as due to her depth perception being affected, she perceived this area as a hole in the flooring. I had many 'creative conversations' with Mum when the combination of lights and shadows played with her mind. Sometimes she would become fearful of what she saw and had to be reassured that everything was ok, as I turned her away and distracted her elsewhere.

Driving home I would feel battle weary from our outings.

One of the funny things Mum did during this time, had to do with a wart-like lump on the side of her nose. For as long as I could remember she always had this lump. She decided she wanted it off, so she bought some wart remover. This didn't work but her nose became so red and painful that we had to see the GP. The doctor then referred us to a specialist. Mum was not happy that we had to wait a couple of weeks to see a specialist. She wanted the wart to be removed straight away, so one day when I arrived at Mum's, I found she had covered the lump with 'Liquid paper'. She now had this large white lump on her face. I tried not to laugh. It was clever in a way. Liquid paper is supposed to cover up mistakes, isn't it?

It's amazing how the mind works.

12

With advice from the Alzheimer's Association I made contact with other carers and attended Support meetings. The facilitators would provide general information, evenings for speakers to visit, discussion on specific topics and above all allowed us time, to talk about what was happening in our lives. As a group we listened, acknowledged hardships and supported each other. Sometimes we could provide an idea or two to help others. Even in those small groups it was obvious, that no two situations were exactly the same. After the meetings I would drive home with mixed emotions, sometimes stopping to have a cry before continuing. I was glad I was able to go for a few sessions.

When I had 'time off', my husband and I would try to go for drives to parks or the beach to relax, walk and spend time together. At home I found watching a comedy relieved the stress. You need to try to keep a sense of humour about the situation and be grateful for things that you have.

Initially I was distressed, that Mum seemed to forget that I was her daughter. She would often refer to me as her friend. I was happy and grateful though, that she still found comfort in our relationship.

It often felt like *Groundhog Day* when I made my daily visits to see Mum. She would be upset because she couldn't find things especially her purse and bankbook. The house would be hot and dark and she would not have eaten. I would open up the house, find her missing items, feed her and talk to her calmly answering the same questions over and over again, day after day.

Mum was obsessive with her purse and bankbook. She swayed between wanting these objects close by, even on her person, to hiding them in a cupboard or under the mattress so no one could take them. Of course a minute or so after they were hidden she would become distressed, crying that someone had taken them. It was then my job to find them.

All Mum's important possessions: her purse, bankbook, pens, scissors, folded pieces of paper and a small torch, which were hidden down her shirt or bra. Two sets of keys were also pinned to her bra straps. It was a funny scene, although for Mum it was very serious. Luckily she didn't have to go through an airport metal detector. Somewhere in her mind she knew she was forgetting things. She was frightened of what could happen to her and her home, so she furiously clung to her precious belongings.

Also at this time Mum's health and behaviour were affected by the medication she was or wasn't taking. Although I would give her the night tablets before I left in the evening, sometimes she would rediscover her tablets in the *Webster pack* later in the night and take more. It's a wonder nothing serious happened.

At the Memory Clinic it was decided not to continue with the medicated patches she was wearing, as they were giving her too many side effects. This was to be Mum's last visit as they could no longer slow down her memory loss.

Mum had no sense of time, the passing of time, telling the time and day/ night appropriate courtesies. I suppose everything appeared cloudy to her. She was ringing constantly from 4pm to 2am and they were not always happy calls. The speed dial button on the phone was being overworked. Even after spending the whole day with Mum, as soon as I left her driveway, she would ring my phone. She was lonely.

After working the early morning shift I would bring a special treat over for Mum to eat. She loved her piece of fish and a potato scallop. As long as I sat down to eat with her she would attempt to eat. 'Meals on Wheels' were cancelled as Mum didn't want strangers coming into her house, plus she wasn't eating their food.

We had bought Mum a new TV, a digital one and most days I would carry the TV out to the lounge and turn it on. She would not sit in front of it for very long. She complained that the TV was too noisy, too bright or it was a *"stupid show anyway"*. Using the remote was very confusing and frustrating for her. On most nights Mum would put the new TV away and bring the old heavy TV back out. This often left bruises on her arms from the effort. The old TV was not digital and did not work.

Conversations with Mum were more like a repetitive series of questions and answers. As the afternoon wore on, Mum would become more agitated. I would encourage her to have a bath and put on her pyjamas once it became dark. Mum would only have a *'birdbath'* and then sometimes it was just her face. I would cook a simple dinner as invariably nothing would be eaten. Sitting at the dinner table with Mum, was like waiting for a young child to finish eating their vegetables. At about 9:00pm after several checking and rechecking of the locks on the doors and windows, and finding her torches, of which she had four, I left for the night. Mum would call during the night with everything that was happening.

We decided that I would begin staying at Mum's initially for three to four days in a week. This did calm her down especially at night. I was still working full-time on the early shift, which was probably the best one to have in the circumstances. At least I could be with Mum during the dreaded afternoon and evening sessions. If Mum was going to sleep at all, she would sleep a couple of hours from 4am on, which was when I would leave for work. During my lunch break I would ring to see how she was and reassure her that I would soon be there. Evenings and night time was when Mum was most active and most distressed, opening and closing doors, cutting up papers, looking for things as well as walking around and around.

Mum's quality of life was spiraling rapidly downwards.

13

"Bring it back NOW and everything else you have taken!"

"I don't think I've got it ... I don't know ... ... everything just goes away ... I can't remember where things are after I've found them"

"Is this still my house? Do I still live here?"

"What do I do? ... ... No one has told me what to do. Do I just sit and wait for someone to come ... someone to make my food, someone to help me? And you're NOT going to take it away from me!"

"Oh forgot what I had to say ... Oh ... bills ... ... I have to get some money. How does it come about?"

"I wish my back would stop crying.."

"I'm missing something. I'm writing it all down so I can understand."

"I could stand outside and scream! I've had a shit of a day."

"I just want to stand out on the road and wait for a bus to come." (and hit her)

"I've got to get out of this house or I'll go mad."

Time and time again Mum's late night calls would begin like this.

A decision as to her care needed to be made.

I had been in contact with Centrelink to find out about Aged care living, procedures and potential costs. It was a depressing minefield. Various forms and phone calls later a Statement of Value of Assets for Residential Aged Care Providers was calculated by Centrelink. They had valued Mum's home.

As I scoured the internet, looking at websites and glossy magazines it was like learning a new language as I tried to comprehend what an Accommodation Bond, Exit Statement and Management Fees were.

Visiting some of these facilities shook me to the core. The fragrance of strong, antiseptic and bleach were often used as an attempt to cover other musty smells which also hovered in the air. Patients limited by various physical and mental capabilities would turn their heads towards the door as I, the uninitiated, would enter their large recreation areas. On realizing that I was not someone familiar, they would then turn their disappointed faces and slump back into their chairs. The loneliness I felt emanating from them was very difficult to handle. Was I putting Mum in this situation? How could I? Surely I could continue caring for her, couldn't I? The feeling of guilt was immense.

My husband lent his support and came with me to view the homes. Some places had secured Dementia areas, others didn't. As Mum had started wandering, the security was essential. They all however, had long waiting lists. Mum's name was placed on our top four.

Mum's physical wellbeing was also deteriorating now. She had always worked in the yard and walked down to the shop quite easily, but now she walked with a slow shuffle. Her balance was also being affected. She slowly moved down the hallway of her house using her hand as a guide on the wall as she went. A fall from off a step ladder a few years prior, was now giving her considerable pain. She also had other health issues. She no longer understood that she needed to rest her body, eat sufficiently and drink water more frequently to help her body.

Mum now swayed between states of depression where she would cry or think of ending it all, to fits of suspicious paranoia and anger.

Many Dementia sufferers recall memories from their youth. On the rare occasions Mum would recall her Dad and his beloved dog that would wait all day beside his bicycle whilst her Dad caught the ferry across the river to work at the Murrarie 'Meatworks'. She would talk about the 'kids' or 'the boys'. Whilst cleaning the house, she would give 'the boys' a rag mat each to sit on and they would scuttle across the wooden floors providing a polish to the floor in the process. The doors to other parts of Mum's memory remained closed, secret. I would try to open some memories with stories I recalled, but all too often they were met in clouded silence.

Driving home one day, I was alerted to an advertisement on the radio. There was an 'Open House' event for a series of new aged care facilities that had 24/7 Aged and Dementia care. Arranging an appointment, I visited the displays. They seemed ideal. Small three-roomed units, only a few steps away from a large eating / recreational area. They seemed to tick all the boxes on quality living and ongoing health care. The sale of Mum's house would provide the funds for the costs, plus they had two units available now.

At last! This was the answer to my prayers. The unit was like a small house. There were people who would provide meals, cleaning, a variety of activities, and administer necessary medical requirements. Family could visit whenever they wanted. It was only a couple of blocks away from where my husband and I lived as well as close to Mum's great grandchildren's school.

Ideal, but how could I tell Mum?

How do I move her out of her home that was hers for the last fifty years of her life? This was going to be hard.

It was actually Mum's rantings that initiated the difficult conversation that I had to have with her, and then repeat it several times later. She started to say:

"I've got to get out of this house.

I want to sell this house.

I'll go back home."

Although not sure which home she was referring to, I pushed on regardless. I agreed with her that selling the house and moving to a smaller place was a good idea.

Using all the positives I could think of and avoiding using the term, 'moving into a home or nursing home', Mum seemed to calm down. The following night we again had the same conversation, but I came prepared with photos of the easy to manage units.

Striking 'while the iron was hot' I took Mum firstly to a coffee shop that was situated in a 'home' to give her the feeling of how other people lived. We did however avoid any large signage to the 'home'. After a *'cuppa'* I drove Mum to the intended 'unit'. It was a morning where Mum seemed relaxed. I was so grateful for this. Mum gave a positive remark about the unit. I felt so happy, so relieved. The necessary paperwork was signed and a deposit organized.

It was now five years since Mum's bowel cancer operation.

14

Mid 2011

Now the implications of signing the *'99 year lease'* for the unit for Mum were being felt. Setting up a Real Estate agent to come into Mum's house and look around was tricky. The 'home' had recommended the agent, as Mum's house had to be sold within a certain time frame for their contract. We thought *'no worries'* as earlier in the year houses were selling well in the Brisbane North area. The agent however was only available to inspect Mum's house in the evening.

Oh no! Prime dementia time!

I was as nervous and twitchy as *'a cat on a hot tin roof'*. Every time I heard a car noise I went out to the door. The gods must have been looking on me favourably that night. Waiting by the phone for the outcome, my brother and sister must have also been holding their breaths. Looking back Mum coped fairly well. I was the one with the stress headache.

The agent performed very well, endearing himself to Mum, commenting on her lovely clean house. As I had provided a lot of information about Mum and the house prior to his visit, the discussion about sales figures and costs were kept to a minimum. A contract was drawn up to sell Mum's house.

It was amazing that I didn't crash and burn over the next couple of months. I ran on adrenalin. The real estate market dived. Housing prices plummeted.

I started to try to declutter Mum's clothing. She had lost so much weight, so this seemed an easy place to start clearing out unwanted items.

Like a scene from an old-time comedy, as fast as I was placing clothing into allocated bags, Mum was resorting them, 'helping' me, by pulling them back out again. When I was preparing her garden for the Open House events, Mum would follow me around like a puppy. At one time she tried to move the ladder, whilst I was still on it pruning the trees. These were good times as Mum and I seemed to work together, like old times. The afternoons were always different however.

As the contract deadline crept closer and with no sale, the price on Mum's home had to be slashed drastically. It was finally sold for $100,000 less than the Centrelink valuation.

The next steps were to physically move Mum and empty the house. Most of the furniture would have to be given away or dumped, which would have been heartbreaking for Mum to witness, so we decided to move her into the unit with new smaller furniture, before we turned her home into a discarded shell. Thankfully my brother and sister had arranged to come up to help me take Mum to the unit. They then stayed and cleaned her former home, our family home.

The final week before 'moving day' was horrific. Several times a night I had the same conversations with Mum. She released lashings of anger, anxiety and fear all over me. One night I rang my brother and sister crying, as Mum shouted accusations in the background.

Two days before the move, my sister arrived in Brisbane. Mum didn't know who she was at first. Her memory played tricks on her as she saw *the young girl* walking down her steps. My husband and I spent a very long day moving Mum's belongings into her unit. We waited for furniture to arrive at the unit and then assembled cupboards, a bed and table whilst my sister had 'an interesting' day keeping Mum company. My brother arrived that evening.

Finally the morning arrived for Mum to travel to her new unit. I was so nervous. I felt like I was preparing to leave my only child at school for the first time. My brother and sister were also nervous. They tried to distract Mum.

Sitting quietly in the car with her handbag on her lap Mum looked out the window. What was she thinking? Did she really know what was happening? I just wanted to hold her in my arms.

My husband and daughter met us at the unit complex and together we all went into the meeting area where Mum was welcomed by her Case Manager. After being shown around their facilities, we walked to Mum's unit. My husband and I had worked hard to make it look *'homely'* for Mum. Her favourite statues were displayed along with photos of family. On her bed was a quilt which I had made displaying all our family's faces.

The time came for us to leave. No one wanted to go.

Mum wanted to come with us. Emotions ran high. The drive back to Mum's house was silent, but thoughts of Mum raced through our heads and hearts.

Over the following days we turned to the task of emptying and cleaning Mum's house. My son-in-law came over with a trailer to transport unwanted furniture and tools away. My son and daughter organized items from Grandma's cupboards into various bags and boxes. My brother and sister worked hard cleaning walls, curtains and sorting out remaining items of Mums. My brother, sister and I spent time together recollecting old memories before they had to return to their own homes.

Finally my husband and I cleared the last few items from the house and I spent some quiet time tearfully saying goodbye to the place I also called home. I felt in a way, that I was saying goodbye to my heritage. My father was no longer alive and Mum was almost a stranger. I realized that I possessed a lot of the families' collective memories. I wanted to learn more about my parent's beginnings, so I considered researching our family tree.

15

"I have never seen anyone like your mother.
She doesn't sit down or do as she's told!"

Mum had not settled in well.

Usually when a new resident arrives, they ask the family not to visit for a while, to allow them time to settle into the new routine more easily. However, three days after Mum arrived her Case Manager asked me to come in for a meeting.

I was told that Mum was difficult to care for.

Was I aware that she cried all the time?

Well yes!

All this information had been given to the Case Manager before Mum moved in. She now insisted that I visit Mum every day for six weeks. At that time they would then reassess her. I was very confused. I felt Mum was being regarded as a criminal for *'not following their rules'* and I was to become her prison officer. Due to my work commitments and fatigue I did not see her Sundays. After work in the afternoons I would arrive to see Mum.

Almost running to me she would start crying.

"Can we go home now?"

"This is your home now," I replied

"Well can we go soon?"

It was like a nightmare. What had I done?

The facilities were clean and the nurses I had met seemed friendly. What was I to do? People reassured me that it would be fine. It might take Mum longer to settle in. Medication was prescribed to calm her down. Mum started roaming at night, so a door buzzer was organized. When Mum opened the door of her unit at night, the office of the night attendant would be alerted.

At night feeling distressed and disoriented, Mum would often pack up all her belongings and place them into boxes and sheets, and then drag them outside. This seemed to annoy some of the staff so it was left for me to collect and reorganize back into the cupboards of the unit. A couple of 'Activity Leaders' tried to occupy Mum during the day by giving her small jobs to do, like folding all the napkins for the next meal. This helped Mum feel useful. I thanked them for that.

I would still take Mum out for a *'cuppa'* and we would buy something special for her. The great grandchildren would visit with my daughter once a week. In the care facility, there was a walkway to a garden area where there were some hens in a henhouse. The children liked taking Nanna for a walk there.

As the months passed, the great grandchildren started commenting *"Nanna's different, strange"*. She didn't always respond to their questions. She would walk away from them or she would fall asleep in mid conversation. The children were also noticing that Nanna didn't know basic things like: where the milk was kept as she looked in the bin for it or where the toilet was. It was only a three room unit with the middle room being the toilet bathroom. Mum's actions were becoming so unusual that the great grandchildren were becoming unsettled during their visits.

Mum became incontinent and had to wear nappy-like pants. When she was told to take off her nappy pants she didn't know what to do with them, so she hid them. I would later find them under her pillow, mattress or in her clothing drawers. No one else seemed to notice. Mum started to hand wash some of her dirty clothes, but instead of hanging them on the small outside line or inside on the clothes airer, she would also hide the wet washing.

The stench of wet clothes and smelly nappy pants was so offensive in the unit that I would almost gag as I entered. Again staff failed to notice. On subsequent days, the routine of locating the wet or smelly items, changing bed sheets and then taking all the wet items home to wash, began. Complaining to the Case Manager and the Manager of the Home seemed to make no changes to Mum's care. I was told that caring for Mum was very time consuming. We were quickly learning that the advertised 24/7 care was not accurate. Many of the qualified staff also complained of how little time was allocated, so they could provide *extra* help to residents if they felt there was a need. The more dedicated ones left the home's employment in the short time Mum was there.

Mum seemed to *'pick up'* two similar friends. Together they would always be on the move walking from one place to another. One afternoon I spotted the three of them sitting on a bench just outside the eating area.

They told me they were,
"Just waiting for the bus."
Trying not to giggle, I asked them how long they had been waiting.
"A while. We must have missed the first one!"

When I arrived in the afternoons the carers and some of the other residents seemed happy to see me. Many of them were concerned for Mum.

Mum was no longer going to the lunchroom to eat, as she was too busy walking to sit down and eat. I requested that her lunch be placed into her unit so she could eat it later. However, I would find her lunch still sitting in the fridge in the evening or in the garden outside her door. No one seemed to notice the slices of ham and tomato which would hang on the branches in the garden. As well as collecting all Mum's wet items and returning the dry clothes, I now became the garbage collector. Scattered around the base of the plants I discovered yogurt containers, ice-cream sticks and other packaging from food I had purchased, in the hope it would entice Mum to eat. Several of the nurses knew the extra work I was doing, but they couldn't help me. I continued to complain.

We all thought that once Mum was in care, life would improve for both Mum and me. That was not happening.

The phone rang late one evening to inform me that an ambulance had been called, as Mum had 'taken a turn' and could I meet the ambulance at the hospital. No more information was provided. Racing to the hospital, I waited an hour before I could see Mum. She was lying on an ambulance stretcher in the corridor still waiting to be seen. It was a busy night. We then waited a few more hours until Mum was admitted. The doctor would see her in the morning. The nurses in the meantime took my details and Mum's blood pressure etc.

The next morning I returned to the hospital to find Mum roughly secured to the bed. Mum was upset to say the least. A nurse came over explaining that they had tied Mum up, as she would constantly get up and move away from her bed. They thought it strange that Mum did not know where she was, or where she lived, although at the top of her folder in large print were the words DEMENTIA. The 'home' had not sent any paperwork, so they didn't know why Mum was there or her current medication. After tests, it was revealed that Mum had a Urinary infection. These are quite common amongst the elderly and they play havoc with their health.

After a couple of days Mum was released from hospital care. It took about a week for Mum to recover from the anxiety of being unwell and in hospital. Mum however, developed diarrhea due to the continuation of her hospital medication. I found her one day in soiled clothing, so I showered her and cleaned the area. She was very weak and could hardly hold herself up in the shower. I was so upset for Mum. How embarrassed she must have felt to be in this predicament.

Mum's eyes became duller. She didn't really seem to 'settle in'. I had to make a difficult decision, that it was probably better the great grandchildren did not see Nanna for a while. My daughter was upset with the decision, and also with the fact that her beloved Grandma's health was continuing to spiral further downwards.

In my eyes, Mum's level of care was not good enough

as too many disturbing things were happening. I asked again for a new Case Manager. They were now locking Mum in at night. A couple of nurses would return to Mum's unit after their rounds to check in on her.

One evening the nurse was so concerned over Mum's failing condition she called the doctor. He in turn called for an ambulance. I arrived at the hospital and provided my details, which seemed mysteriously to be missing from the information sent from the 'home'. They suspected another urinary infection but they were also concerned about her medication level. Once again after a few days she returned to her unit.

About a fortnight later I received a call at work from my husband saying Mum was in hospital again. They had found her on the floor of her unit during their morning rounds. She had obviously been vomiting all night they said. I was at work when my husband called. I checked my phone and no one from the home had called or left a message for me. Leaving work straight away, I then received a call from the Case Manager, still the original one.

She told me *"I was irresponsible"* as they had not been able to contact me about Mum's condition.

I was furious! My blood boiled. How dare she make that accusation, after all I had been through! All my contact details including work numbers were in their records as I had deliberately double checked this, after Mum's previous hospital visit.

It was nearly 11:00 in the morning by this time. I later put in an official complaint about the Case Manager and Mum's treatment.

At the hospital, Mum was in the care of the same Head nurse as her previous visit. The nurse was very concerned about the rapid decline that had occurred in Mum's health since then.

Mum now had signs of Parkinson's disease. She could hardly move her limbs. She was so stiff. Help in the busy hospital was limited, so I had to take Mum to the toilet. Moving off the bed and walking to the toilet took an eternity. She had loose bowels once again and could not move her arms to wipe her own bottom. I had to do it for her. Poor Mum. What more did she have to go through.

16

May 2012

Lying in her hospital bed
Wrinkled and weary
Where had Mum gone
She seldom smiled
Rarely recognized anyone

Mum had been in hospital for two days when a quietly spoken woman ambled up alongside the bed, asking to speak to me about Mum's condition. Introducing herself as a Liaison officer from Community Health, she wanted to discuss Mum's level of care. Feeling my concern, she arranged an appointment for me to speak with someone who could assist me further. A compassionate gentleman explained that a team of doctors were going to assess Mum as he felt she would now be reclassified as *'high care'*. He also advised I look for another care facility, one that could cater better to Mum's future needs. The 'catch' was that I had to find a place within thirty days as the hospital could only 'hold' a bed for Mum that long.

"When we truly love a person,
It sometimes means,
That we have to push ourselves further,
Than we ever thought were possible."

Receiving leave from work, I visited various high care facilities completing application forms. On the 35th day Mum entered a different nursing facility. With papers signed, her old unit was emptied and a room in her new 'home' was filled with Mum's belongings. We were ready for a new start.

Mid-morning on Mum's first day in the home I received a phone call from the nursing staff to say Mum had had a couple of falls in the garden, nothing serious, just a cut on the forehead. The Director of the home remarked,

"I didn't think she (her Dementia) *was that bad so we have moved Mum.*

We moved her to the secure Dementia wing."

This is where initially I wanted Mum to go but they had no beds.

"We hope this is alright with you.

Will you be coming around this afternoon so we can have a chat?"

I thought, *"Oh no, here we go again."*

17

Carers

Being a carer is such a physical and emotionally demanding job. We do it because we love them, simple and true.

I was Mum's daughter. I can't begin to think how much more complex it must be for a husband, lover, parent or partner with a young family. How do they cope? How do they feel? Some carers receive physical as well as verbal abuse which is another level of difficulty to contend with. Support groups, respite care and a strong family friendship base is essential. Taking time out even if only briefly, to relax, to laugh and to be 'normal' is very important. Accept the time out and return refreshed.

As the sufferer becomes increasingly frustrated, anxious, angry and lost this is when they need more of your love, support and understanding. Carers often report that one of the most irritating symptoms sufferers have, is to ask the same question over and over again. We need to try and not to argue with them, but gently reassure or distract them. I know this is tough. Even leaving the room may be best for both parties. Don't curse yourself for getting angry as being a carer is rigorous. No one is perfect. We are all human. So for the tenth time try to answer that same question.

It is very important that carers take care of their own health. If you became ill, injured or in hospital who would care for them? Sometimes an emergency plan needs to be organized. As well as the carer's health being affected due to the stress of the situation, their other relationships can be stretched to breaking point. The carer spends a lot of time and energy with the Dementia sufferer. Communication with other family members and friends is of paramount importance also. My own relationship with my husband was certainly over stretched.

18

June 2012

After Mum's initial falls at her new home, she seemed to settle fairly quickly into a routine. When I entered the Dementia wing for the first time it was a little daunting. As the door opened all eyes would turn towards you. Sufferers would frequently shout out their thoughts and their frustrations as you passed by. They also had no real idea of what 'personal space' was, so they would walk right up to your face, especially the men, to speak or 'babble' to you and wait for a response. It did take a bit of getting used to, for both Mum and myself.

The home became part of my life also. The staff became an extended family for both of us. I knew the routine of the day, where the cups and bibs were for meals etc.

After consultation with the doctor assigned to Mum, it was decided to withdraw some of Mum's medication so she wasn't as 'drugged'. He felt some of her previous medication was unnecessary. Mum still continued to cry and have high anxiety but there was more interaction with staff. With less sedative medication it made Mum more alert so she could enjoy the relative freedom of walking around the secure circular garden path.

I felt more relaxed that she was in an area with 24/7 nursing care available. The nursing staff in the Dementia wing were active day and night. They knew when Mum was walking around at night. Being proactive, they would try to convince Mum to return to bed or allow her to sit in a chair to watch TV, where hopefully she would have a snooze. Some days one of the head nurses would take Mum on a longer walk through the other sections of the nursing home as she did her evening rounds. This would help tire Mum out, as well as give her something new to look at or do. I liked the way Mum was introduced to everyone, even in this section of the home. This meant wherever she went, people were aware of who Mum was, and also who I was. For a 'change of scenery' I would often take Mum through the other wings of the home or outside the complex for a walk or sit on the benches.

In Mum's Dementia unit there were the 'walkers' and the 'sitters'. Everyone was encouraged to walk. Walking helped the muscles in the body as well as increasing circulation in the legs and heart. By walking a person may see different things that could stimulate their mind as well as meeting and possibly conversing with others. Some people however remained steadfast, sitting alone in their chair watching the world blur past.

Some days when walking down the hallway it was like 'Grand Central Station' with people and their walkers going backwards and forwards. A few competitive souls would push their walking frames past the 'slower ones' often causing collisions and arguments. Although I bought a frame for Mum to use, she found it difficult 'to drive' and didn't think she required it to walk. She would walk around and around the garden pathway and inside hallway all day every day. This kept her fit but also aided in more weight loss. I am glad however, that she kept walking, as this seemed to be a display of her determination to keep surviving and not give up.

In the home it was noticeable to me that many of the residents, including Mum, liked to collect things, pretty things. Our family would often joke about the latest trinkets our *'bowerbird'* mother had collected. One day on the bedside table I noticed a new photo frame. Inside the frame were two strangers. Obviously Mum thought they looked familiar and possibly friendly so she decided to keep it. No one else seemed to claim them. Outside on her many walks, Mum would collect sticks. She was very particular about the type and size of sticks she chose. Everyone became used to seeing Mum with her bundles of sticks. On days when she was more distressed, the staff would allow her to carry a soft towel, as this seemed to give her some tactile comfort.

It was always difficult for me to leave, as Mum would start crying or hang onto me, but the staff were very good. They would gently take Mum's hand or distract her, so I could leave. This was always very distressing for me and I often left with tears in my eyes. In the later stages, Mum sometimes wouldn't realise that I had left and this would further distress me.

> *Today when I left you I felt sad.*
> *A horrible emptiness engulfed me.*
> *I miss you Mum.*

19

Exiting the Dementia unit was a carefully coordinated procedure as many of the residents would hover around the door. They knew this was a way to get out and that by pushing the keypad, it seemed to unlock the door. A few of the residents would often be seen trying to crack the code on the keypad. After leaving the Dementia wing you would then sign out in the visitor's book. At Mum's previous 'home', they kept no records to show who entered or left the home, including residents. One day I found Mum alone and very distressed crying in their car park. I was so glad that her new home was more secure.

I was still involved with the previous home however. Mum's unit had to be sold by 'their people' before she could receive the money owed to her. We were still paying a monthly fee similar to Body Corp fees. There were Exit Fees to be deducted once it was actually sold. Mum had lived there for less than a year. Due to Mum's vomiting and incontinence in the last weeks she was there, stains were left on the carpet. They could not be removed, so the carpets were replaced and the walls repainted. These costs were also to be deducted from the sale of the unit. It took nearly three years before Mum would receive her money.

As time passed we settled into a routine but emotionally it didn't become any easier for me. Mum started to ask me,

"Where is Deb? (me)

When is she coming?"

I sadly replied that she'd be there soon.

I kept in touch with two of Mum's sisters. Growing up we hardly had contact with Mum's family, which was sad for everyone. I think Mum had a '*falling out'* when she married Dad. Her sisters visited Mum at the previous 'home' and continued to send cards to Mum with loving words. I would read the cards to Mum and reminisce on stories that Mum had once told me about her family. We hoped that this gave Mum a sense of being loved and not being alone. I would often re-read these cards to her.

As a treat I would sometimes take Mum out and meet one of her sisters at the local coffee shop. There the sisters would chat, reminisce and laugh. Mum used short phrases or simple one word responses. Mum's brother in law would often accompany his wife. In times past, Mum enjoyed a friendly banter of name calling with him, so on these more recent occasions he would try to evoke some of her cheeky responses like, "Strewth!" "Bastard." "Well that's typical." Raised eyebrows or 'the look' from Mum made us all laugh as we knew then that Mum was still there, somewhere.

We would take photos to celebrate the occasion. I often used the photos which were stored on my phone, as a tool to initiate conversation and memories with Mum when she stopped walking long enough to sit, talk and rest. Mum didn't rest often and this was also becoming an issue.

Noticeably at this stage, when I arrived to see Mum, she would hardly recognize me. After spending time walking beside her though, 'waffling on' about family, the kids, the weather, the noise of traffic on the other side of the high wooden fence, she would then realise that I was someone she knew. The tone of my voice, the words and phrases I used, or the touch of my hand, stirred a response or memory of closeness.

"Although Mum no longer knew my name,
Did that make me any less important to her?
No!"

Time moved on and I continued to take Mum out. On our last visit to the hairdresser, Mum wouldn't sit still long enough to have all her hair cut. As she stood up and walked to the door, the hairdresser had to quickly 'even up' Mum's hair.

Eating and drinking were proving difficult also. I would order two small milkshakes and a piece of cake which could be eaten with our fingers, plus lots of napkins. Using a straw was easier for Mum than juggling a hot cup of coffee.

Mum liked to carry a purse when she went out. It no longer held any cards or money though, just small pieces of paper and maybe a comb. It was no longer a purse that belonged to someone with a familiar identity. Similarly Mum seemed just a faded watermark of who she once was.

Moving Mum in and out of the car became more difficult, as she didn't seem to know how to sit down into the car and turn her legs around. I started to half lift her in and out. The Director of the Home noticed this and gave me a piece of plastic for the seat. I used this to try and swivel Mum's legs around in the car. It worked partially, but with some sadness I had to stop taking Mum out.

Her grasp of the English language was slipping. Often numbers were interlaced with words, half words and sounds. At times she would softly utter something and then look at me for an answer. Depending on the tone with which it was delivered, I would fabricate some form of reply. This created another chasm between us. On the wall in Mum's room was a canvas which I had decorated with pictures of the family. Each photo was named, so the staff could also try to initiate conversation with Mum.

The shape of Mum's face changed. Holding her jaws clenched, her small thin face emphasized her large brown sad eyes.

Balance and co-ordination started to affect Mum's walking. On some days she would walk differently to other days. In the hallway she was advised to hold the rail as a guide, but *'Miss Independence'* hardly listened and she seemed to deliberately walk down the centre of the space. She started to take a few tumbles, falling in the garden area as well as inside. Large bruises including black eyes and cuts would now cover Mum's sad face. Her beautiful soft olive skin showed signs of struggle.

One day I received a phone call saying that Mum had assaulted another patient and that their family was lodging a formal complaint. Reminiscent of when a school Principal calls a parent into their office over a child's misbehaviour, I sat in the Director's office. I rallied to Mum's defence, as although Mum could be feisty, this was unusual behaviour for her.

Mum started running a temperature a couple of days later. They suspected a urinary infection and Mum was sent to the hospital. This they thought could also explain Mum's earlier aggressive behaviour.

Arriving at the hospital I found Mum in the psychiatric ward firmly tied to a chair.

Déjà vu.

I was furious and demanded to speak to a nurse. A staff member from administration arrived to apologize and ironically explained some new procedures that were being *'rolled out'* for dementia patients. This was so they could receive extra care and sensitivity. Well they weren't working! Mum was moved to another ward, but she still needed to be restrained from walking around and becoming lost or possibly injured. Every morning they would wait until I arrived. They would then release Mum so that I could give her some medication, as she was refusing to take it and feed her. This distracted her long enough so that they could take her blood pressure etcetera. They were long days for me. Luckily I had taken leave from work while Mum was in hospital. As she was quite thin a Nutritionist came to visit Mum and together *they* discussed her eating habits. Her food requirements arrived, but the packaging was difficult for Mum to remove and the food awkward to eat. Obviously the memo about the needs of dementia patients hadn't arrived in that department either.

As Mum's dementia advanced other medical issues arose. After one of her falls the doctor suspected a fractured nose or cheekbone but due to her stage of dementia, x-rays were out of the question. Mum could not follow any instructions, especially to stay still. Similarly Mum had a 'turn' where an MRI would normally have been undertaken. They contemplated anesthetizing Mum to keep her still in the MRI machine, but at that stage they didn't think she would survive the anesthetic.

20

I am who I am
I know I seem different
But love me,
Accept me,
For who I am now.

Two years had passed and we helped Mum celebrate her 80th birthday with milk drinks and cake. Emotionally I was struggling at this stage because I was becoming physically isolated from Mum. As her daughter, I longed for Mum's touch. It hurt to accept that the staff at the home, were more like family to her. I knew most of the staff by name. They were friendly and also supported me.

I warmly referred to the other patients as the 'inmates'. New inmates arrived, still somewhat alert, but slowly over time changes would occur. Bandages would appear on their limbs, skin tears, black eyes, wet pants, and with clothes hanging off their tiny bodies they would sit dribbling, with vacant pale faces waiting for visitors, for help, for peace.

They would often call out to me when I arrived,

asking for help to aid them in walking or to answer a question. Many of the original inmates had left. It was noticeable when someone passed on and another 'newbie' arrived. *"Did we look that scared when we first started?"* I also started to wonder how things would end for Mum.

After a couple more falls it was agreed that Mum should wear a skull cap similar to that worn by footballers to protect her head. She already wore padding on her hips in the sides of her pants for protection.

The Doctor called for a meeting where some difficult questions were asked. On Mum's 'Advance Health Directive', which had been completed some four years prior, she had stated that in the event of accident or other health issues she did not want to be resuscitated. The doctor went through the repercussions of this statement with me as they were concerned about the number of falls Mum was having, as well as the amount of pain she was experiencing. I had to decide if Mum should receive a significant increase in medication which would ease the pain and slow her down. This would confine her to a bed or chair and therefore she would not have as many falls. The alternative was to allow a small increase in medication which would allow Mum to continue walking knowing that the next fall could be fatal.

Oh boy!

Although a difficult decision to me it seemed a clear choice. I decided that Mum would not want to be confined to bed. She would want to have some freedom for the remainder of her life. She would continue to walk. After the meeting, I held myself together until I reached the car where I then proceeded to *'bawl my eyes out'*. That night I contacted my family to tell them of the decision.

21

Walking was not an option today
As she sits restrained in her chair
I look into her faded brown eyes
My frail grey haired Mum cries
Her thoughts no longer her own
Trapped in her clouded world

Mum continued to have good days and bad. Every three months I would give consent for chemical (another sedative) and physical restraint to be applied if needed. This allowed a calming tablet to be given if Mum became too distressed in the evening.

Mum was walking quickly, too fast, and as she was travelling in a bent over position this meant there was a higher percentage rate of Mum falling. To slow her down, as well as provide her with some rest, they would place her in a chair with a tray, which could be locked into place. This was similar to that of a baby's high chair. Of course she didn't like this, but it was for her own good. Often she would be 'released' when I arrived.

Mum was like our own 'Energiser bunny'. Whenever she had a fall or was ill, a day or so later she would pick herself up and start her walking routine again. Throughout her life Mum tried to instill in us a strong sense of resilience and work ethic. I'm sure her beliefs in this, is what kept her going for so long.

On rare occasions a spark of the old Mum would shine through. One day when I arrived for a visit, a tall dark haired young male attendant called me over. Looking for sympathy, he told me that Mum had slapped him. I smiled as the vision of this very tall young man being harassed by my tiny bent over grey-haired mother appeared in my mind. I replied, *"Well did you deserve it?"* Surprised he shook his head, '*like mother like daughter*'. Evidently he had greeted Mum in a cheeky manner and Mum replied with a quick slap. It was a sign of her playful affection. I was overjoyed. Mum was still there.

Sometimes quite suddenly my day would receive a huge boost, when Mum would stretch up from her stooped position and look me straight in the eye with clear brown eyes. It was as if she knew who I was. It was an euphoric feeling. Somewhere deep inside my Mum still knew me.

Good news arrived in late November. The settlement of the unit at Mum's previous home was finally complete. The timing of this sudden influx of money couldn't have been better, as payment of Mum's fees were becoming a concern, another stress.

My journey with Mum and dementia was often very difficult and lonely. She went through many changes both physically and in personality. My role changed as I became more like a mother to Mum. It was challenging. To come to terms mentally with this, I referred to

Mum's changes as the various facets of a diamond. I began to feel privileged that I was able to see my precious sometimes raw and multi-faceted mother change. Dementia doesn't always destroy a person's humanity and kindness. Often facets of personality can still appear and glimmer in the darkness. I think my brother and sister missed out a lot, by not having the opportunity to see Mum still shine near the end of her journey.

22

2015. Another year begins.

In the middle of January Mum's breathing became more laboured and she started having more difficulty walking. Mum was using the rail in the hallway. I was guiding, holding Mum's arms to walk around. We would pause often. It was like she was forgetting how to move her legs. She was falling out of her bed as the message from her brain to her legs was not connecting quickly enough for her to stand up. This was scary. I asked the doctor what was happening. He gently told me that she was in the final stages.

"What did that mean?"

She still looked relatively normal, her normal.

February 2015

A week later I noticed Mum was having trouble swallowing. I called the doctor. The following day Mum could not swallow liquids. The nursing staff were looking at me through sad eyes. I knew this was not good. With tears in my eyes I spoke to a nurse that had become a good friend. She told me that once they can't swallow, it wasn't long.

I cried.

That night I called all the family and gave them the terrible news. One of Mum's sisters and her husband came up the following day. It was a particularly difficult morning for Mum. The Nurses had placed Mum in a chair supported by pillows while they tried to feed fluids into her failing body. The fluids just dribbled back over her crusty lips. She had no strength to support herself in the upright position. I felt helpless but I had to stay strong, now more than ever before. They placed Mum into her bed and gave her morphine.

The following afternoon, my children and some of my grandchildren came to visit Mum. The younger ones sensed something was wrong. My daughter found it extremely difficult to leave Mum's bedside. My son remained deep in his thoughts as he tried to hold his emotions together in the confined space. I think I was in a daze. I felt scared. There was so much to say, so many feelings.

Another granddaughter of Mum's who was living in Brisbane, spent time alone with Mum, talking to her, holding her hand and playing her favourite music.

That afternoon my brother arrived. I was so glad to have him there by my side. It was also my birthday.

My sister couldn't come up but gave me a message to tell Mum,

"It's ok. You can relax. You can let go now. I love you."

Mum opened her eyes and seemed to nod slightly.

I cried again.

Mum lay there so fragile and so precious. She was

using all her energy to breathe. She looked so frail. I tried to remember everything I saw and felt about Mum.

In the early hours of the following morning my phone rang with an unfamiliar voice softly saying,

"She has gone."

Still groggy from disrupted sleep, I couldn't comprehend, so I asked her to repeat it.

Mum had gone.

Mum had held on until she had seen or heard from everyone.

On the day after my birthday, Mum took her last breath.

It was a final gift to me from her.

Thank you Mum.

23

Feeling numb, I woke my daughter and her husband to tell them. Four months earlier I had separated from my husband. I had been staying with my daughter's family. My daughter and I drove to the motel where my brother was staying and silently we drove to see Mum for the last time.

I was scared to see Mum now.

Even in her final moments Mum must have fought for life as she did not look at peace. I reacted with anger. Surely she could have been given a peaceful ending after her long struggle?

I tried to console myself, that this way it highlighted Mum's courage and determination.

As we had paid previously for a funeral plan, this simplified the final process and the relevant people were contacted. My daughter, my brother and I waited with Mum until they took her away. Quickly and quietly we bagged up the remainder of Mum's belongings and crept out of the nursing home, just as a new day was starting.

"Just as parents bring their newborn child into the world
It is the children's job to help parents leave our world with grace and dignity."

I don't think I fully grieved for Mum at that time as there was still so much to organize. I wanted the service to reflect the beautiful, caring woman that she was. It was important that the service was from all of us and it had to be something Mum would approve of.

The day of the funeral passed by in a blur. There was family I hadn't seen for a very long time, all friendly and supportive. Many of the staff from the nursing home came as a tribute to Mum. She was very much loved.

I believe that when a person dies their soul stays around for a short time to watch over their loved ones, to help them cope. Often family and friends report that they 'feel', receive signs, or in dreams their dear departed appears to them. Memories, favourite songs, a cheeky grin, expressive hands, the sight of familiar grey hair or the feeling of a touch often evoke images of Mum to me.

Throughout the years I found writing in my journal was a way of expressing my feelings. Every now and then I still write a letter to Mum or to both my parents telling them the news of the family. By reaching out in this way I find peace.

24

After a loved one's passing, a hole is left not just for them but also for the routine, the home, and the people that formed so much of your lives for many years, but life goes on. It has to.

Dementia still remains a part of my life. My ears prick when welcome news is reported that a cure for Dementia may be close. I have participated in Charity walks for Dementia. I know of other people who volunteer their time within the organization or at Nursing homes.

As a legacy to Mum, if this book can help at least one person then I will feel that Mum's final years had purpose.

In loving memory
Now at peace
Treasured and loved
By all she touched
Forever in our hearts

Notes of Interest

Dementia can strike anyone: hard working everyday people, high flying executives, highly skilled workers, scholars, artists, former athletes, the elderly and unfortunately younger adults.

Figures updated on fightdementia.org.au website in February 2017 indicated that there were more than 413,106 Australians living with Dementia. By 2025 the number of people with dementia in Australia is expected to increase to 536,164[2]. Triple these figures and you have the number of people living with and being affected by a Dementia sufferer. Scary statistics. These are not just statistics however, they are very real people with families trying to cope and live with this diagnosis.

Dementia describes a collection of symptoms that are caused by disorders affecting the brain. Dementia is not one specific disease. Most people with dementia are older but it is NOT a normal part of aging. Currently Dementia is the second leading cause of death in Australia[3] with no miracle cures. As preventative measures, researchers do

---

[2] Alzheimers Australia website
[3] Alzheimers Australia website

encourage everyone to maintain healthy eating, sleep, exercise patterns and social interactions throughout our life whilst learning new skills to encourage brain growth.

Mental functioning declines and affects a person's memory, intellect, understanding and the ability to perform everyday tasks. The exact symptoms will depend on the areas of the brain damaged by the disease/s. As the initial disease progresses it is not uncommon for the individual to be diagnosed with an overlap of diseases eg Vascular Alzheimer's. In many cases the damage is caused when normal nerve cells stop communicating and functioning with other brain cells and die. Nutrients to other nerve cells can also be interrupted when clumps or tangles formed from insoluable plaques are created within the brain. This plaque is similar to that which builds up in our arteries and leads to our hearts. High blood pressure and cholesterol are risk factors of Dementia.

The diagnosis of Dementia can often leave the sufferer and family with feelings of helplessness and depression. Dementia can bring families together trying to support each other or it can also increase the strain or stress within families and relationships.

When given the diagnosis of Dementia we often think about the final stages of dementia where a person cannot speak or eat, but that may not be for several years. It affects everyone differently. Planning for the future is very important for the mental, physical and financial future of the sufferer as well as the spouse, children and family that remains.

Many 'care facilities', respite and nursing homes encourage their residents to participate in a wide range of activities. Sensory gardens, excursions, community sing a-longs, bingo sessions, visits from young people and furry animals are becoming a normal event in many facilities.

One of the most important roles for a carer is to continue to provide a quality of life for the sufferer. Planning short outings to meet family members, helping in the garden or workshop, enjoying nature, playing familiar music, games or even starting up a new hobby with them, can help them create new memories and so enjoy their life further.

This journey may take several years, so it is important that the carer also looks after themselves.

There are over 100 diseases that may cause dementia.[4] Some of the most common causes of dementia are Alzheimer's disease, Vascular dementia, Lewy body disease and Frontotemporal dementia sometimes called Pick's disease. If you are diagnosed before the age of 65 you are said to have Younger or Early-onset dementia. Australian statistics updated in February 2017 stated there were an estimated 25,938 people with Younger onset dementia[5].

Dementia in younger people can be very aggressive. The rapid decline of these sufferers, has a devastating impact on their families. It is heartbreaking to watch these young people who in the prime of their lives with such promising futures and often with young families, try to cope with their fatal diagnosis. To add to this heartbreak

---

[4] Alzheimers Australia website
[5] Alzheimers Australia website

is the inadequate number of facilities available to cater for younger sufferers. Normally dementia patients would be cared for in an aged care or nursing home.

The symptoms and stages of Dementia vary from one individual to the next depending on which parts of the brain are affected and the severity of the damage.

When doctors first meet individuals or worried family members who are concerned about a change in memory or behaviour, they first have to discount other conditions which may have symptoms similar to Dementia. These conditions could be vitamin or hormone changes, infections, side effects of medications, depression or tumours. Most of these conditions are treatable. Depression though can be interweaved with Dementia.

Doctors will discuss current medical and lifestyle history with the patient. This can be difficult to collect if the patient is worried that they have the beginnings of dementia and so cover up the frequency of the symptoms or even deny their occurrence. A patient may not be a regular visitor to a medical office and so a thorough health assessment is necessary.

A physical examination is given with blood and urine tests taken to investigate levels of iron, electrolyte balances, vitamin B12 deficiency, liver and thyroid functions as well as infection and medication problems. A short test which consists of a series of questions can be used by the doctor to assess the patient's cognitive or thinking abilities. An example of this is the MMSE or Mini–Mental State Examination. This simple test is used to measure memory, concentration, spatial awareness, problem solving, counting and language skills.

Further testing can also be undertaken such as standard x-rays, brain scans, MRIs and more involved testing of memory and comprehension. Images of the brain can indicate loss of brain tissue, areas of disease and previous damage due to accidents or strokes. This assessment can be conducted by your doctor or from a specialist doctor such as a geriatrician, neurologist or psychiatrist. A diagnosis of Dementia is given when two or more cognitive functions are affected.

Alzheimer's disease is the most common form of dementia. About 70% of Dementia sufferers have this disease. Short term memory loss is often the first noticeable symptom but over time a person has difficulty finding the right words for common objects. Familiar everyday tasks such as dressing, using cutlery and making a cup of tea take longer and become difficult to perform. As the disease progresses they become frightened, angry and easily disoriented. At the end stage of the disease it is common for the sufferer to no longer recognize close family members. They become reliant on carers for basic daily eating and hygiene activities.

Vascular dementia is the broad term for dementia associated with problems of circulation of the blood to the brain[6]. A single stroke or several small strokes or TIAs (transient ischaemic attacks) can damage the brain affecting cognitive thinking which interferes with daily functioning. Symptoms vary depending where and how much of the brain has been affected. Some small TIAs can't always be detected due to the area or depth of the

---

[6] Alzheimers Australia website

brain affected. A sufferer my not know they have had a mini stroke. They may only remember picking themselves up off the ground and not recalling how or why they fell. Sometimes they may have only a bad headache with no fall involved.

Lewy body disease is caused by the degeneration and death of nerve cells in the brain[7]. In short periods of time a sufferer can change from appearing normal to severe confusion as well as disruptions to attention span and thinking processes. Visual hallucinations are a common symptom of this disease.

When the symptoms of movement are affected first, **Parkinson's disease** is often diagnosed. As Parkinson's disease progresses, people often develop dementia. Overlapping disorders such as Dementia with Lewy bodies, Parkinson's disease dementia, Lewy body disease with Alzheimer's/Vascular dementia evolve. As more of the brain degenerates more symptoms are detected from other diseases.

Frontotemporal dementia or Pick's disease as the name implies, is where the frontal and /or temporal lobes of the brain are damaged. The frontal lobe affects our behaviour and personality whereas damage to the temporal lobes involves language problems such as finding the right words, remembering people's names, speaking fluently and understanding the meaning of words. Sufferers with this form of dementia often exhibit socially inappropriate behaviour as they appear compulsive, aggressive or rude.

---

[7] Alzheimers Australia website

Acknowledgements

With love and gratitude I would like to acknowledge all the special people, including family, friends and associates who assisted and supported me throughout the formation of this book. The idea formed in my mind several years ago and with the ceaseless encouragement from loved ones and the possible celestial guidance of my parents, this book materialized.

Thank you to the second, third and fourth set of eyes who looked over the various editions of my manuscript. Special mention goes to the *Beta reader* and library staff who assisted me in the initial editing arena. Balboa Press my publishers, provided me with the vehicle and assistance to bring the story into fruition. Thank you for your updates and support.

Writing this story was such an emotional process for me. It reminded me of all the other untold stories I heard, the other 'inmates' as I lovingly called them, their carers, their families, my family and the enormous amount of compassionate workers both in the health industry as well as office workers who helped Mum and I. Certainly we had stumbling blocks along the way, but that only made us more determined.

Forgive me for not personally listing everyone, as I was worried I would leave someone out.

Warm thanks goes to all the staff who work in the 'Homes'. I am deeply grateful for the care and attention given to Mum by the nursing staff. They helped me through many difficult times.

Finally, to the people behind the websites and organizations, who contribute to the wealth of information we have at our fingertips, the voices at the other end of the often teary phone calls, the people involved in setting up respites, fund raising and awareness campaigns and the scientists who are forging ahead in their important research, I applaud and encourage you to continue this fight against dementia.

Thank you

Websites to begin your search:

Alzheimersaustralia
fightdementia.org.au
qld.fightdementia.org.au
www.myagedcare.gov.au

The websites provided many resources:

- factual information
- help sheets
- support and services
- education and consulting
- research and publications
- further resources
- What's On – State by state
- Social media feeds
- Newsletters
- National Dementia Hotline Helpline 1800 100 500

Other organizations and staff which were helpful:

Community Health
Meals on Wheels
Centrelink
ANZ bank
Post office staff
AVEO
Local government representative

About the Author

Debbie Flack the eldest of three, is a mother, grandmother and ex teacher with 30 years' experience. She enjoys escaping suburbia for the tranquility of nature where she reads and pursues her passions of art and photography.

Printed in the United States
By Bookmasters